AMAZING NFL STORIES
12 HIGHLIGHTS FROM NFL HISTORY

North Paulding High School
300 North Paulding Dr.
Dallas, GA 30132

by Matt Scheff

www.12StoryLibrary.com

12-Story Library is an imprint of Peterson Publishing Company and Press Room Editions.

Produced for 12-Story Library by Red Line Editorial

Photographs ©: NFL Photos/AP Images, cover, 1, 14, 18, 20, 29; Pro Football Hall of Fame/ AP Images, 4; Paul Sancya/AP Images, 6; Fort Worth Star-Telegram/AP Images, 7; AP Images, 8, 10, 12; Action Sports Photography/Shutterstock Images, 9; Photography Plus via Williamson Stealth Media Solutions/AP Images, 11; Charlie Krupa/AP Images, 16; Rusty Kennedy/AP Images, 17, 22, 28; Jacquelyn Martin/AP Images, 19; Neftali/Shutterstock Images, 23; Rick Osentoski/AP Images, 24, 26

ISBN
978-1-63235-151-7 (hardcover)
978-1-63235-191-3 (paperback)
978-1-62143-243-2 (hosted ebook)

Library of Congress Control Number: 2015934296

Printed in the United States of America
St. Louis, MO
March, 2017

Go beyond the book. Get free, up-to-date content on this topic at 12StoryLibrary.com.

TABLE OF CONTENTS

1

THE NFL RISES FROM HUMBLE BEGINNINGS

Today's National Football League (NFL) is a spectacle. No pro sport is bigger in the United States.

The stars are big. The money is bigger. Yet the league's beginnings were quite small.

Akron Pros players around 1921

By 1920, pro teams were scattered around the Midwest. There was no single champion. There was no shared rule book. Players went to the highest bidder. It was chaos.

Ralph Hay owned one such team, the Canton Bulldogs. Hay thought he had a better way to operate.

So in 1920, he invited several other owners to his car dealership in Canton, Ohio. There, the men agreed to form the American Professional Football Association (APFA). They later renamed it the National Football League.

The early NFL didn't look much like the league we know. Most of the teams were from the Midwest. They didn't play a fixed schedule. Most still played against non-NFL teams. There were no playoffs or championship game. Teams voted for the 1920 NFL champion four months after the season. The Akron Pros ended up with that belated honor after an 8–0–3 season.

14

Teams in the NFL's first season in 1920.

- The NFL was called the American Professional Football Association in 1920 and 1921.
- Only two of the original NFL teams still exist. The Decatur Staleys are the present-day Chicago Bears. The Racine Cardinals are today's Arizona Cardinals.
- The Dayton Triangles won the first game between two NFL teams. They beat the Columbus Panhandles 14–0 on October 3, 1920.

ANOTHER NFL FIRST

The first televised NFL game was on October 22, 1939. An estimated 500 viewers watched the Brooklyn Dodgers beat the Philadelphia Eagles 23–14. No footage of that first broadcast exists today.

2

THANKSGIVING DAY GAMES BECOME A TRADITION

Turkey. Stuffing. Mashed potatoes. Family. They're all staples of most Thanksgiving Day celebrations. So is football. The NFL has been playing Thanksgiving Day games since 1920. In the coming years, Thanksgiving football would provide fans with plenty of thrills. In 1980, the Detroit Lions and Chicago Bears played the first Thanksgiving overtime game. The Bears' Dave Williams returned the opening kickoff 95 yards for a touchdown to end it.

In 1993, the Dallas Cowboys appeared to be on their way to a victory over the Miami Dolphins. The Cowboys blocked a kick with seconds to go. It should have been over. But Dallas defensive lineman Leon Lett chased down and touched the ball. That made the ball live. Miami recovered and kicked the game-winning field goal.

Detroit Lions fans tailgate with a turkey before the 2011 Thanksgiving game.

The Dallas Cowboys' Leon Lett loses the ball against the Miami Dolphins on Thanksgiving in 1993.

Confusion reigned in 1998. The Lions and the Pittsburgh Steelers went to overtime. Steelers running back Jerome Bettis called "tails" for the coin toss. The toss came up tails, but referee Phil Luckett misunderstood. He gave Detroit the ball. The Lions went on to kick a game-winning field goal.

And who could forget 2012? New York Jets quarterback Mark Sanchez made blooper reels everywhere. He ran right into the rear end of one of his linemen. Then he fumbled! Sanchez's "butt fumble" remains one of the most amusing plays in NFL history.

84

Total points scored in a 1986 Thanksgiving game. The Green Bay Packers outlasted the Detroit Lions 44–40.

- The NFL has held three games every Thanksgiving since 2006.
- The Dallas Cowboys and Detroit Lions traditionally host Thanksgiving games each year.

PLAYERS TAKE THE FIELD WITHOUT HELMETS

Modern NFL helmets are wonders of engineering. They have high-tech padding, sensors, and shock absorbers. They're the most important piece of safety equipment in the game. Yet early on, many NFL players didn't even wear helmets. Those who did wore soft leather helmets that offered little protection. Harder plastic helmets came to the NFL in 1939. By this time, most players were wearing some helmet.

The last man to step onto an NFL field with no helmet was Chicago Bears running back Dick Plasman. Plasman had suffered a head injury just two seasons before. Yet he still took the field for the 1940 NFL Championship Game without a

Washington Redskins quarterback Sammy Baugh shows off his helmet in 1945.

4

Pieces of safety equipment required by the NFL: a helmet and shoulder, thigh, and knee pads. Players can wear additional pads if they choose.

- The chin strap was invented in 1940.
- The single face bar appeared in 1955. A fuller face mask was introduced 21 years later.

THINK ABOUT IT

Would you want an NFL career if you knew it meant you might suffer brain damage? Is the fame and money worth it?

Modern helmets offer better protection against head injuries.

helmet. He and the Bears won the game 73–0. Soon after, the NFL passed a rule requiring helmets for all players. However, Plasman was allowed to go without a helmet until 1947.

Modern-day players have grown concerned about the effects of the game on their brains. Many players have suffered one or more concussions. These brain injuries can cause long-term damage. Concussions are common despite modern helmets. One can only wonder what kind of damage was done to those early players who didn't have any protection at all.

THE NFL GOES TO WAR

Football and other sports took a backseat in the early 1940s. World War II raged in Europe and on the Pacific Ocean. Millions of US men went to fight for their country. Athletes were no exception. More than 1,000 NFL players and coaches served in the military. They included legends such as George Halas, Norm Van Brocklin, and Chuck Bednarik.

Not all of them came back. Among the 23 killed was tackle Al Blozis. He died in France just six weeks after playing in the 1944 NFL Championship Game.

Owners faced a player shortage. Teams scrambled to fill rosters. In 1943, the Bears convinced former great Bronko Nagurski to play again. He had been retired since 1937.

Chicago Bears star Bronko Nagurski in 1943

23

NFLers killed in action during World War II. This included 21 players, one coach, and one front office member.

- Not every team managed to fill a roster. The Cleveland Rams suspended play entirely in 1943.
- The combined Chicago Cardinals and Pittsburgh Steelers team was called Card-Pitt.
- World War II lasted from 1939–45.

The Pittsburgh Steelers and Philadelphia Eagles had another idea. The two Pennsylvania teams merged. They formed the "Steagles" in 1943. The following year, the Steelers again merged, this time with the Chicago Cardinals.

THE TRADITION LIVES ON

In 2002, Arizona Cardinals safety Pat Tillman was a rising star in the league. Tillman was set to make millions of dollars on his next contract. Yet he turned it all down. Tillman enlisted in the US Army. He became a Ranger and went to Afghanistan to fight. Tillman was killed in 2004.

US Army Ranger Pat Tillman in 2003

5

ONE GAME CHANGES EVERYTHING

The NFL was popular during the 1950s. Yet it was nothing like it is today. Many experts point to the 1958 NFL Championship Game as the turning point. It's been called "The Greatest Game Ever Played."

Baltimore Colts fullback Alan Ameche scores the winning touchdown in the 1958 NFL Championship Game.

45 million

Estimated TV viewers of the 1958 NFL Championship Game.

- The 1958 NFL Championship was the first NFL game to be telecast nationally.
- The game was also the first ever to go into overtime.

The game was telecast on NBC. Viewers were in for a treat. It was a dramatic battle between the Baltimore Colts and the New York Giants. Quarterback Johnny Unitas led the Colts to a last-minute field goal to tie it. Overtime! Fullback Alan Ameche scored in overtime to give the Colts a thrilling victory.

The game marked the beginning of a new era for the NFL. Experts have credited it with sparking a new level of interest in football. TV ratings soared. A rival pro league formed.

STALL TACTICS

Late in the fourth quarter of the 1958 title game, the Baltimore Colts had the ball on the New York Giants' 8-yard line. A huge play loomed. Suddenly, the TV feed blinked out. Viewers nationwide saw only static. That's when someone ran out onto the field. Most thought it was just a crazy fan. Police chased the man up and down the field. The delay was long enough that the TV audience didn't miss much. Only later did the truth come out. It was not just a crazy fan who ran onto the field. It was NBC employee Stan Rotkiewicz. He was stalling so the network could get the game back on the air.

Within a decade, the Super Bowl was born. The Super Bowl has gone on to become the biggest TV event of the year. And none of it might have happened if not for one thrilling game.

A RIVAL LEAGUE CHALLENGES THE NFL

The NFL was booming in the late 1950s. Wealthy individuals around the nation were begging to be granted expansion teams. Yet most were turned away. So in 1960, some of these men started their own professional league. The American Football League (AFL) made an instant splash.

AFL owners spent freely to attract players. The NFL owners were not

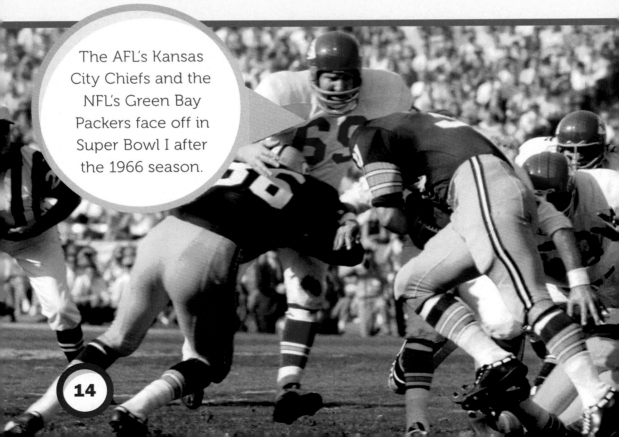

The AFL's Kansas City Chiefs and the NFL's Green Bay Packers face off in Super Bowl I after the 1966 season.

pleased. They did all they could to squash the new league. When the AFL planned to place teams in Minneapolis and Dallas, the NFL moved quickly. It awarded expansion teams to each of those cities. The Minnesota Vikings and Dallas Cowboys were born.

Fans were slow to embrace the new league. Yet the AFL soon drew a loyal following. In the end, it was about the players. The AFL offered huge contracts to entice NFL players to switch leagues. The NFL responded in kind. Salaries skyrocketed. The competition between the leagues grew until 1966. That's when they agreed to merge. The AFL-NFL World Championship Game would become known as the Super Bowl. The rest is history.

10
Present-day NFL teams that began in the AFL. They are the Bengals, Bills, Broncos, Chargers, Chiefs, Dolphins, Jets, Patriots, Raiders, and Titans.

- The AFL-NFL merger was finally completed in 1970.
- The Houston Oilers won the first AFL Championship in 1960, then won again in 1961.

BROADWAY JOE LEADS THE AFL TO RESPECTABILITY

The NFL dominated the first two Super Bowls. Many fans and media criticized the AFL. They said that the league was not as good as the NFL. Then came Super Bowl III. The AFL's New York Jets were huge underdogs to the NFL's Baltimore Colts. But brash quarterback Joe Namath guaranteed a victory for his Jets. "Broadway Joe" and the Jets delivered with a stunning upset. Then the next year, the AFL's Kansas City Chiefs defeated the NFL's Minnesota Vikings. That put to rest any idea that the AFL was the weaker league.

15

THE SUPER BOWL JUST GETS BIGGER

The first Super Bowl wasn't even called the Super Bowl. It was the AFL-NFL World Championship Game. And it was far from the spectacle it is today. The NFL champion Green Bay Packers crushed the Kansas City Chiefs 35–10. The message was clear. The NFL still ruled.

That first Super Bowl in January 1967 was a success. Both CBS and NBC showed the game on TV. They attracted 51.1 million viewers. NBC collected between $37,500 and $42,500 for each 30-second ad. The event only got bigger. Today, the game is an international affair.

More than 100,000 fans attended Super Bowl XLV after the 2010 season. The Green Bay Packers beat the Pittsburgh Steelers.

For many, the Super Bowl is as much about the sideshows as the game itself. Television commercials have become must-see TV. In 2015, companies shelled out a whopping $4.5 million for 30 seconds of ad time. The halftime show is just as big. Early on, Super Bowl halftime shows were often simple marching band performances. The bar was raised in 1993. That's when pop icon Michael Jackson took the stage. Jackson's show was a ratings smash. Since then, the biggest stars in music have headlined the halftime show.

114.4 million

US viewers who watched Super Bowl XLIX on TV in 2015, a record.

- The largest crowd to attend a Super Bowl was 103,985.
- That game, Super Bowl XIV, was held in January 1980 in Pasadena, California.

THINK ABOUT IT

The Super Bowl would never have been born if the AFL hadn't formed. How different might the NFL be today if the AFL had never existed? Would it be as popular?

THE DOLPHINS STAND ALONE

Perfection. It's the goal of every NFL team. Yet only one team has achieved a perfect season.

Most people expected the 1972 Miami Dolphins to be good. A year earlier, they'd gone 10–3–1 and lost the Super Bowl to the Dallas Cowboys. The 1972 season started out with five straight wins. But the fifth came with a price. Star quarterback Bob Griese was injured. He missed the rest of the regular season. Yet the Dolphins just kept winning. They used their smothering "No Name Defense" to crush one opponent after the next.

The Dolphins kept rolling in the postseason. They won tight games over the Cleveland Browns and Pittsburgh Steelers to advance

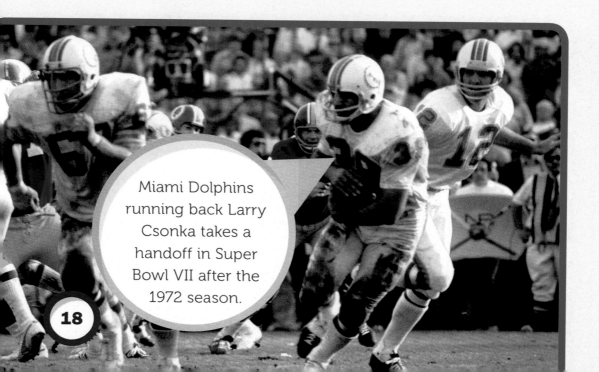

Miami Dolphins running back Larry Csonka takes a handoff in Super Bowl VII after the 1972 season.

Members of the undefeated 1972 Dolphins pose with President Barack Obama in 2013.

to the Super Bowl. There, they outlasted the Washington Redskins 14–7. The win gave the Dolphins a mark of 17–0 on the season and the honor of being the only perfect team in NFL history.

Others have come close. The 1934 Chicago Bears went 13–0, only to lose the NFL Championship Game. The Bears had another shot eight years later but again lost their final game. Then in 2007, the New England Patriots cruised to a 16–0 regular season. The Patriots were heavy favorites to complete the perfect season in the Super Bowl. Yet the underdog New York Giants pulled off an upset to leave the 1972 Dolphins alone on top.

27.5–12.2

The Dolphins' average score during the 1972 regular season. They outscored opponents 385–171.

- The Dolphins finished the season ranked first in the NFL in both offense and defense.
- Larry Csonka and Mercury Morris both rushed for at least 1,000 yards in 1972. They became the first teammates to do so.
- Bob Griese returned in time to start the Super Bowl.

WEATHER PLAYS A ROLE

Wind. Rain. Snow. No other major team sport faces the elements quite like the NFL. Many northern NFL teams play outdoors. That means bad weather can turn a team's game plans upside down.

The 1934 Chicago Bears lost their perfect season on a frozen New York field, when the Giants switched from cleats to basketball shoes at halftime to get better grip on the ground.

The Chicago Bears offense lines up in the fog during the 1988 "Fog Bowl."

109

Degrees Fahrenheit (43°C) when the Philadelphia Eagles played at the Dallas Cowboys in 2000.

- The temperature on the turf was nearly 150 (66°C).

Then there was the 1967 NFL Championship Game. This game is better known as "The Ice Bowl." The wind chill measured a brutal -48 degrees Fahrenheit (-44°C) as the Green Bay Packers and Dallas Cowboys kicked off. A spot in the Super Bowl was on the line. The hometown Packers won on a last-minute touchdown, leaving the Cowboys out in the cold.

Twenty-one years later, a thick fog rolled over Chicago's Soldier Field. The fog was so heavy that the Philadelphia Eagles and Bears on the field couldn't see the sidelines. The coaches couldn't follow the action either. The officials had to tell them what had happened after every play. Eagles quarterback Randall Cunningham passed for

PLAYING THE WIND

Wind has long been a factor in NFL games. It can make passing difficult and kicking nearly impossible. In 2005, the Chicago Bears and San Francisco 49ers played in one of the windiest games on record. Gusts measured at up to 47 miles per hour (76 km/h). Yet the 49ers tried a 52-yard field goal near the end of the first half. The kick wasn't close, and Chicago returned it 108 yards for a touchdown.

407 yards. However, he also threw three interceptions and no touchdowns as the Eagles lost.

It's not just the northern climate that gets in the way. In 1979, the Tampa Bay Buccaneers hosted the Kansas City Chiefs. Rain poured down on Tampa. The field was covered in water and mud. Players struggled to hold onto the slippery ball. The only score of the day was a 19-yard Tampa Bay field goal.

TWO-SPORT STARS SHINE IN THE NFL

The NFL boasts some of the world's best athletes. Many of them excel at more than just football. Legendary quarterback Otto Graham played pro basketball before joining the Cleveland Browns. Chicago Bears wide receiver Willie Gault qualified for the US Olympic track team. Running back Herschel Walker was a member of the 1992 US Olympic bobsled team.

One man took it to a new level in the late 1980s. Bo Jackson was an All-Star outfielder for the Kansas City Royals. He was also one of the most dangerous running backs in the NFL for the Los Angeles Raiders. In the end Jackson's body could not hold up to the two-sport punishment. Both of his careers were cut short.

"Neon" Deion Sanders stepped up to take the role of the world's biggest two-sport star. In 1989, Sanders debuted as a rookie outfielder

Deion Sanders scores a touchdown for the Dallas Cowboys in a 1998 game.

for the New York Yankees and a cornerback for the Atlanta Falcons. In early September, Sanders cranked out a home run for the Yankees and scored a touchdown for the Falcons—all in the same week. It's a record that may never be broken. Sanders went on to become a Pro Football Hall of Famer. Some call him the greatest cornerback in history.

Jim Thorpe on a US postage stamp

Jim Thorpe

USA 20c

2,782

NFL rushing yards gained by Bo Jackson. A hip injury forced him to retire after just four seasons.

- Deion Sanders is the only athlete to play in both a World Series and a Super Bowl.
- Sanders was also a return specialist. He scored nine career touchdowns on kick and punt returns during his career.

JIM THORPE

The original multisport athlete was Jim Thorpe. Thorpe was a football legend even before the NFL existed. He also played major league baseball and ran track and field. Thorpe won both the decathlon and pentathlon at the 1912 Olympic Games. When the NFL formed in 1920, owners voted Thorpe as the league's first president.

NFL SALARIES BLOW UP

Calvin Johnson makes a touchdown catch for the Detroit Lions in 2014.

Today's NFL salaries are mind-boggling. Some of the best players sign contracts worth $100 million or more. That wasn't always the case. For most early pro players, football was little more than a part-time job. The first record of a player being paid dates back to 1892. The Allegheny Athletic Association paid William "Pudge" Heffelfinger $500 to play for them. Pro football was born.

In 1925, college football's biggest star was Red Grange of the University of Illinois. The Chicago Bears gave Grange an unheard-of contract of $100,000 to join their team.

The formation of the AFL in 1960 changed everything. Suddenly, the NFL had competition for the world's best players. Bidding wars broke out. Salaries skyrocketed. The best example was quarterback Joe Namath. Namath was a first-round pick in both the AFL and NFL. The bidding war was on. Namath signed with the AFL's New York Jets

$420,000

Minimum salary for NFL rookies in 2014. It's the lowest total any NFL player could be paid that year.

- Each NFL team operates under a salary cap.
- In 2014, the NFL salary cap was $133 million. No team was allowed to spend more on players.

for a staggering $427,000. Two years later, the leagues agreed to a merger, largely to control salaries.

As NFL free agency has evolved and the NFL's TV revenue has soared, so have NFL salaries. In 2004, quarterback Peyton Manning earned a jaw-dropping $35 million. That's more than $2 million per game. In 2012, Detroit Lions receiver Calvin Johnson signed an eight-year contract worth $132 million. It was the largest contract in NFL history. Salaries only seem to go higher.

TELEVISION LEADS THE WAY

For years, the only way to see an NFL game was in person. That began to change in the 1950s. TV broadcasts gave fans a new way to watch games. Since then, the growth of TV and the NFL have gone hand-in-hand.

In 1960, Pete Rozelle took over as NFL commissioner. Rozelle thought TV was the future of the game. One of his early goals was to have every NFL game televised. Soon, networks were bidding against each other for pro football. Rozelle helped push

A cameraman shoots a 2013 NFL game for FOX TV.

THINK ABOUT IT

Some people prefer to watch NFL games at home on their TVs. NFL teams have tried to make attending games more appealing by adding bigger scoreboards and more technology. Do you think this is the right approach? What changes would you make to NFL stadiums to improve the experience?

$1.9 billion

Amount the ESPN network pays yearly for the rights to broadcast *Monday Night Football*.

- CBS used 62 different cameras to cover Super Bowl XLVII in 2013. That's about five times the number for a standard regular-season game.
- TV even plays a role on the field. The NFL began using instant replay to review certain calls in 1986.

the NFL's next stroke of genius, *Monday Night Football*, in 1970. It soon became the centerpiece of the weekly broadcast schedule. Ratings soared. So did revenue.

The experience has improved for fans as well. High-definition TV became common in homes in the 2000s. Fans were treated to large, crystal-clear pictures. Some fans thought watching at home was better than actually being at the stadium. Don't feel too bad for NFL owners, though. In 2013, every NFL team earned $131 million in TV revenue.

TWO CHANNELS SHOW SUPER BOWL I

In 1966, NBC had the rights to all of the AFL games. CBS had the rights to the NFL games. When the first Super Bowl came along, neither network was willing to step aside. So both of them telecast the game.

FUN FACTS AND STORIES

- The combined 1944 Chicago Cardinals-Pittsburgh Steelers team was called Card-Pitt. The only thing worse than the name might have been the team itself. They went 0–10. Fans mocked them, calling them the Carpets.

- The AFL was the most successful rival league to the NFL, but it hasn't been the only one. The United States Football League (USFL) played three seasons, from 1983–1985. The USFL featured stars such as Steve Young, Herschel Walker, Jim Kelly, and Doug Flutie.

- In one of the first Thanksgiving games, the Decatur Staleys beat the Chicago Tigers 6–0. Rumors swirled that the owners had made a bet. The losing team would have to disband. The Tigers played again three days later. Then they never played again. In fact, there's no record that the Tigers were ever officially part of the NFL. Yet they played seven games against NFL teams in 1920, so historians usually include them as an NFL team.

- The United States is by far the biggest market for the NFL, but it's not alone. Super Bowl XLIX in 2015 was broadcast in 180 countries and in 25 different languages.

- Two current teams played in the NFL's first season in 1920. They are the Arizona Cardinals and Chicago Bears. Both began in Chicago. The Bears were originally called the Decatur Staleys. They became the Bears in 1922. The Cardinals have always had that nickname. They moved to St. Louis in 1960. The Cardinals finally ended up in Arizona in 1988.

- The Cardinals moved twice before settling in Arizona. Other NFL teams have a long history of moving, too. After 22 years in Oakland, the Raiders played in Los Angeles from 1982 through 1994. Then they moved back to Oakland. Meanwhile, the St. Louis Rams spent most of their history in Los Angeles. They played there from 1946 to 1994. Yet the team actually began in 1937 in Cleveland.

GLOSSARY

belated
After the fact.

commissioner
The person who runs a sports league.

concussion
A brain injury caused by a jolt to the head.

contract
A legal agreement between two parties. In football, contracts usually determine a player's salary and how long he will play for a team.

enlist
To join the armed forces.

expansion team
A new team added to an existing league.

free agency
The process by which veteran players can shop their services to any team.

merge
The joining of two leagues or companies.

revenue
Income generated by a business.

rookie
A first-year player.

salary
The amount of money someone is paid for doing a job.

wind chill
A figure that combines temperature and wind speed to measure how cold air actually feels on the skin.

FOR MORE INFORMATION

Books

Howell, Brian. *Football.* Minneapolis, MN: Abdo Publishing, 2012.

Rausch, David. *National Football League.* Minneapolis, MN: Bellwether Media, 2014.

Wilner, Barry. *The Super Bowl.* Minneapolis, MN: Abdo Publishing, 2013.

Websites

NFL Rush
www.nflrush.com

Pro Football Hall of Fame
www.profootballhof.com

Pro Football Reference
www.pro-football-reference.com

Sports Illustrated Kids
www.sikids.com

INDEX

About the Author

Matt Scheff is an artist and author living in Alaska. He enjoys mountain climbing, deep-sea fishing, and curling up with his two Siberian huskies to watch football.

READ MORE FROM 12-STORY LIBRARY

Every 12-Story Library book is available in many formats, including Amazon Kindle and Apple iBooks. For more information, visit your device's store or 12StoryLibrary.com.